Airport

A Cherrytree Book

Designed and produced by
A S Publishing

First published 1989
by Cherrytree Press Ltd
a subsidiary of
The Chivers Company Ltd
Windsor Bridge Road
Bath, Avon BA2 3AX

British Library Cataloguing in Publication Data

Amos, Janine
To the airport.
I. Title II. Lowe, Peter
III. Series
387.7'36

ISBN 0 7451 5071 3

Printed in Italy by Imago Publishing Ltd

Let's go to the
Airport

By Janine Amos
Illustrated by Peter Lowe

CHERRYTREE BOOKS

planes
terminal
buses

Every day people fly on aeroplanes. Some of them are going on their holidays. Some of them are making business trips. Wherever they are going, their journey starts and ends at an airport.

Let's go and see what happens at an airport.

We arrive at the terminal building. It is very busy. There are lots of buses and taxis there. People are carrying suitcases or pushing trolleys.

airport manager

Inside the terminal, we meet the airport manager. He is in charge of all the people who work at the airport. He has to make sure that everything runs smoothly.

Planes fly all over the world from this airport. One plane takes off every four minutes.

The manager shows us a plan of the airport. He points out the terminal building.

Near the terminal there is a huge car park. People leave their cars there, while they are away.

Behind the terminal, there is a runway. Planes take off from them and land on them. A tall control tower in the middle controls all the planes. Nearby there are huge sheds called hangars. The planes are kept in them when they are not flying.

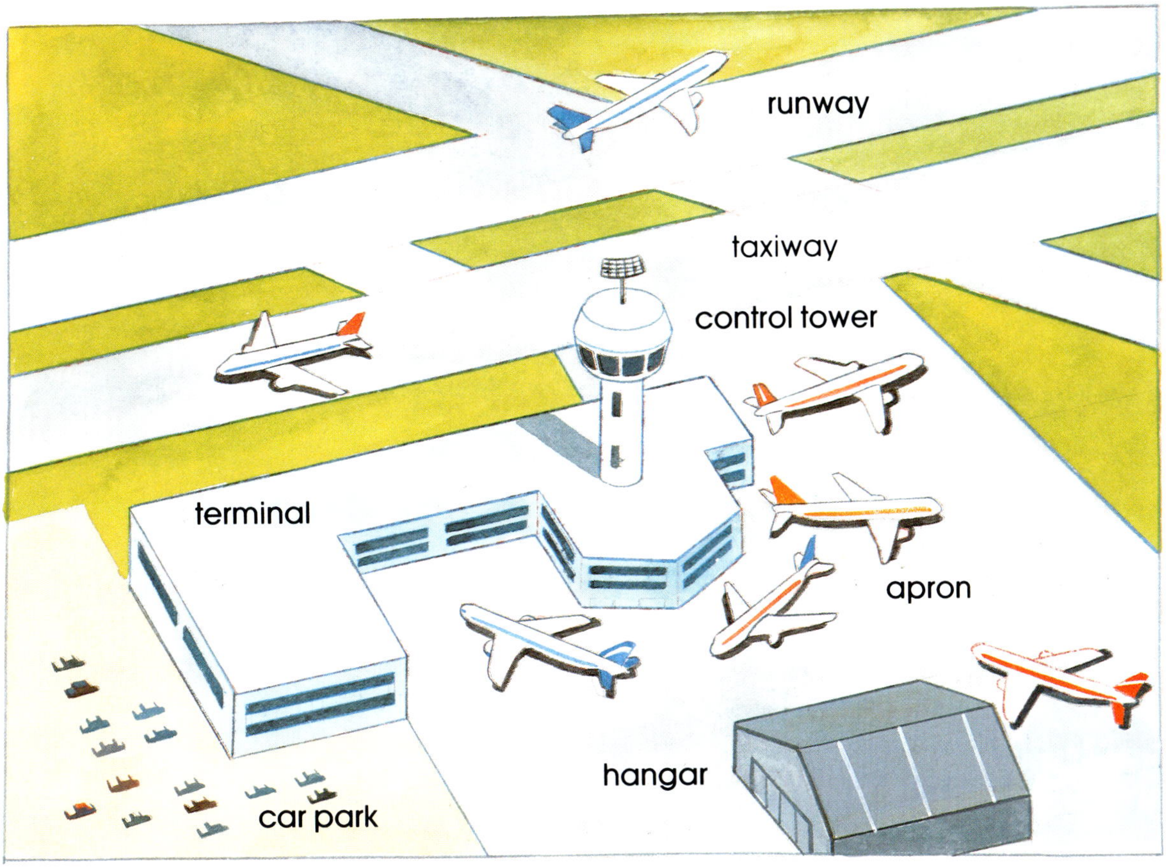

display screen
luggage trolley

We see round the terminal. It is noisy and exciting. People have trolleys piled high with cases. They ask questions at the information desk. They look at the times of flights on display screens. They all seem to be in a hurry.

The terminal is like a small town. There are shops and restaurants, post boxes, telephones and a bank. Some people are going to other countries. They need to change their money.

Many people are standing in queues. They are passengers waiting to check in. They give their tickets to the staff at the check-in desk. The check-in staff weigh the luggage and label it. Then it goes on a moving belt to be loaded on to the plane. Each passenger gets a boarding card. This allows them on to their plane.

departure lounge

The passengers often have to wait until their plane is ready. They may go to the shops and buy a book to read on the plane. They may have a cup of coffee in the restaurant. Whatever they do, they keep an eye on the screens. When their flight is displayed they have to be ready to board. They also listen for announcements from loudspeakers.

If there is time, people can go outside and watch the planes. There is a special observation deck. It has a good view of the runway.

You can see the planes in their parking places. These are called stands. One plane is on the runway. It goes faster and faster and faster. Then it takes off. You can see its wheels.

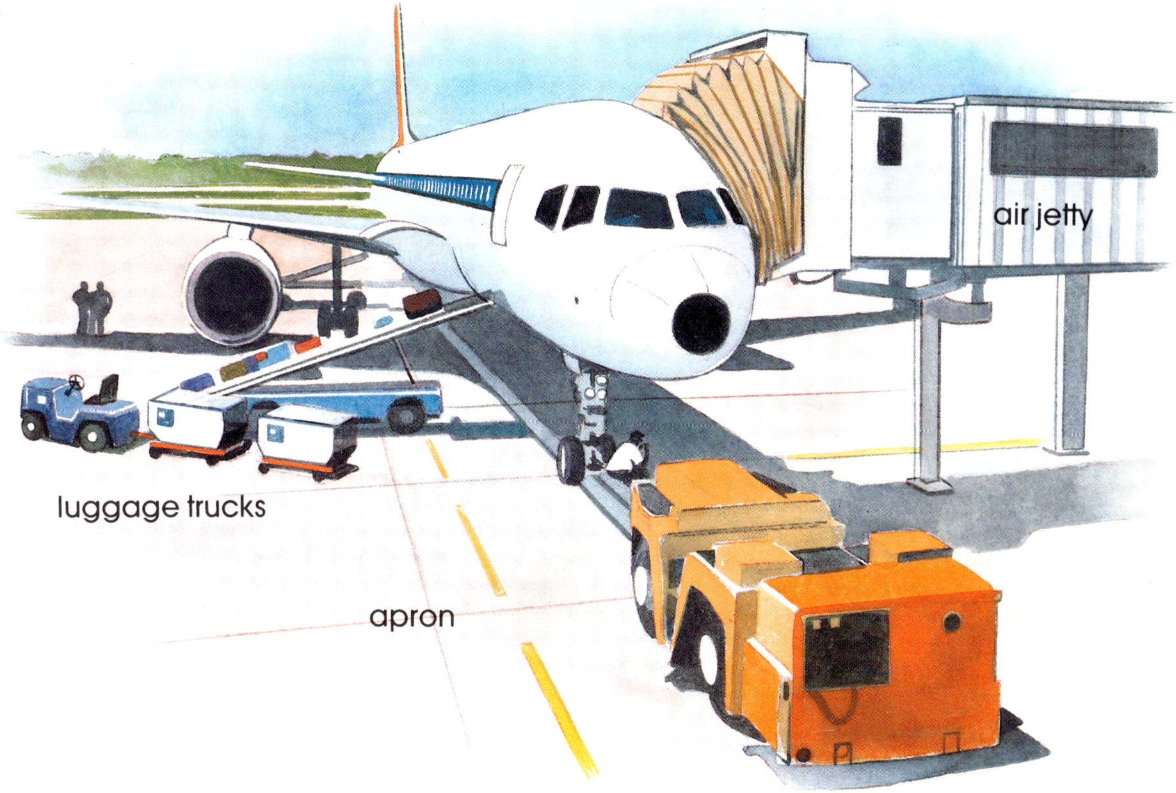

Another plane has just landed. It goes slowly right up to the terminal. An air jetty comes out to meet the plane. The passengers walk through it.

The luggage comes down a ramp. Trucks take it to the terminal. Cleaners go on board to get the plane ready for its next flight. Engineers check every part of the plane.

fuel pipe
loaders
apron

The area where the plane waits is called the apron.

The passengers' luggage is loaded into the hold. There may be mail and other cargo as well.

Food for the passengers' meals is loaded into the cabin. The meals are in sealed containers.

The plane takes on fuel from a pipe. The fuel is in big tanks under the ground.

When it is ready, the plane taxies to the gate

Inside the airport the crew of the plane are getting ready. The captain has a flight plan. It tells him where the plane is going. It gives details of the route. It also tells him how fast to fly.

The captain collects a weather report. If bad weather is expected, he may not be able to land. He may need extra fuel to go on to another airport.

The captain goes through the plan with his crew. He points out any problems for them to watch for. Then the flight crew boards the plane.

The crew make their pre-flight checks. Everything must work perfectly. There are many controls on the flight deck. The plane cannot leave the ground if there is anything wrong.

Before the people get on the plane, they have to be checked, too. This is the work of the security staff. They search people and luggage for guns or bombs.

The passengers walk through a special gateway. If they are carrying anything made of metal an alarm sounds. Passengers' passports may also be looked at.

The staff check all the hand luggage. People put their handbags or briefcases on to a moving belt. This takes the bags through a scanning machine. The machine x-rays the bags. The person checking the bags can see on a screen the shape of what is inside them.

After they have been checked, the passengers go to the gate. The plane is waiting for them.

security screen

control tower

The passengers board the plane. The captain and his co-pilot talk to the control tower. The air traffic controllers tell them which runway they can use.

The plane taxies to the runway. Then it waits for its turn to take off.

The air traffic controllers are in contact with all the planes. Some are landing. Some are taking off. Others are waiting for permission to land or take off.

The controllers guide each plane. They can see in all directions from the tower. They also have a huge panel of instruments. They can see planes in the air on their radar screens. Each one shows up as a blip of light.

air traffic controllers

Take-off and landing are the most dangerous parts of each flight. The control tower keeps in touch with the emergency services. Fire engines are ready in case anything goes wrong.

The runways are lined with lights. They help pilots land safely at night and when it is foggy.

When a plane lands, the passengers walk to the terminal. Trucks bring their luggage to the baggage hall. The cases arrive in the baggage hall on a moving belt. The belt goes round and round, so that all the people can pick up their luggage. It is called a carousel.

There are trolleys for people to put heavy bags on.

customs

Everyone who has been out of the country has to go through customs. You are not allowed to bring some things into the country. You have to pay tax on some other things.

Customs officers make sure you do not smuggle things in. They may search your case. They may search you.

It is not only people who fly from airports. Planes carry cargo as well. Some planes only carry cargo. The goods that they carry are stored in large hangars.

Loading the planes is a difficult job. The cargo must not be too heavy. Its weight must be spread evenly in the cargo hold.

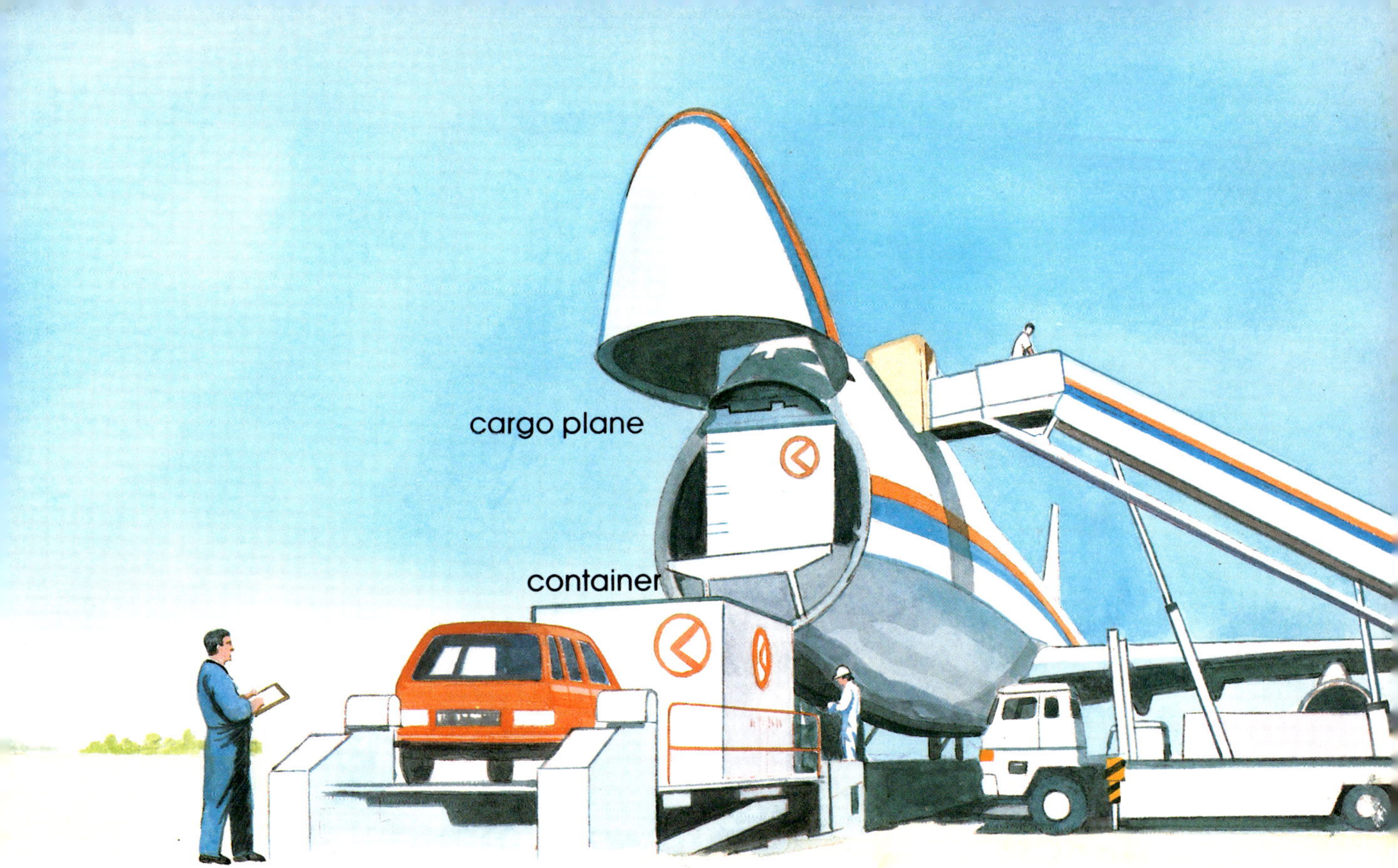

Most goods are packed into large metal boxes called containers. Some are the size of a lorry. Special lifts raise them up into the hold.

It is expensive to send goods by plane. So people mostly send only things that cannot travel slowly. Fruit and flowers spoil quickly. So they are often sent by plane.

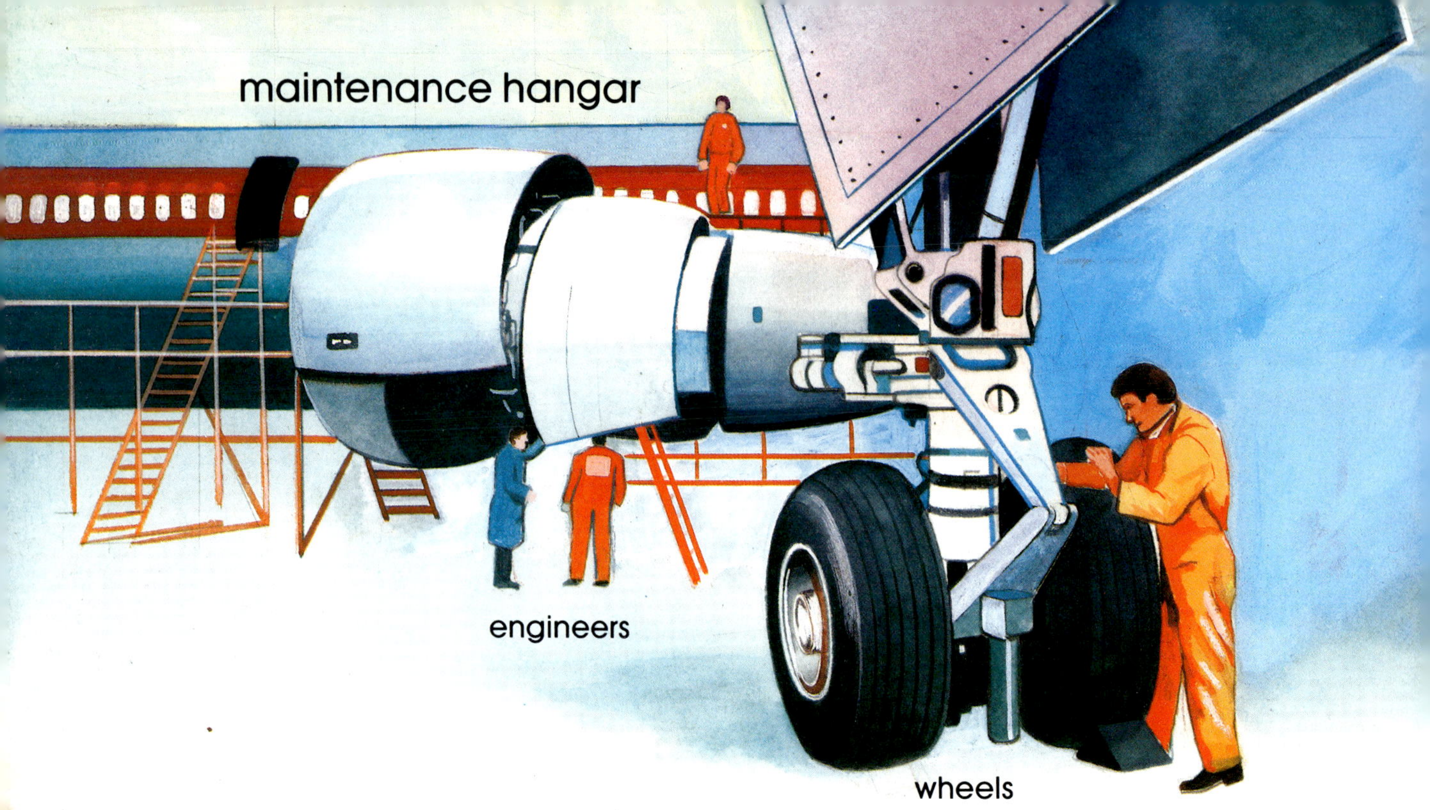

Planes do not fly all the time. After it has flown a certain number of hours each plane is examined. It goes to the maintenance hangar. Skilled engineers look at the engines and every moving part. They check the controls and all the electrical systems.

They x-ray the body and wings to make sure that there are no tiny cracks. They replace parts before they have a chance to wear out.

We watch the engineers working in the hangar. Once everything is all right, the planes can fly again. One plane is ready. They wheel it outside.

Now we have seen everything at the airport, we can go home. The airport manager gives us each a Fact File which answers our questions. Then he gives us a surprise. We are going up in the aeroplane. Now we shall see the airport from the sky.

Fact File

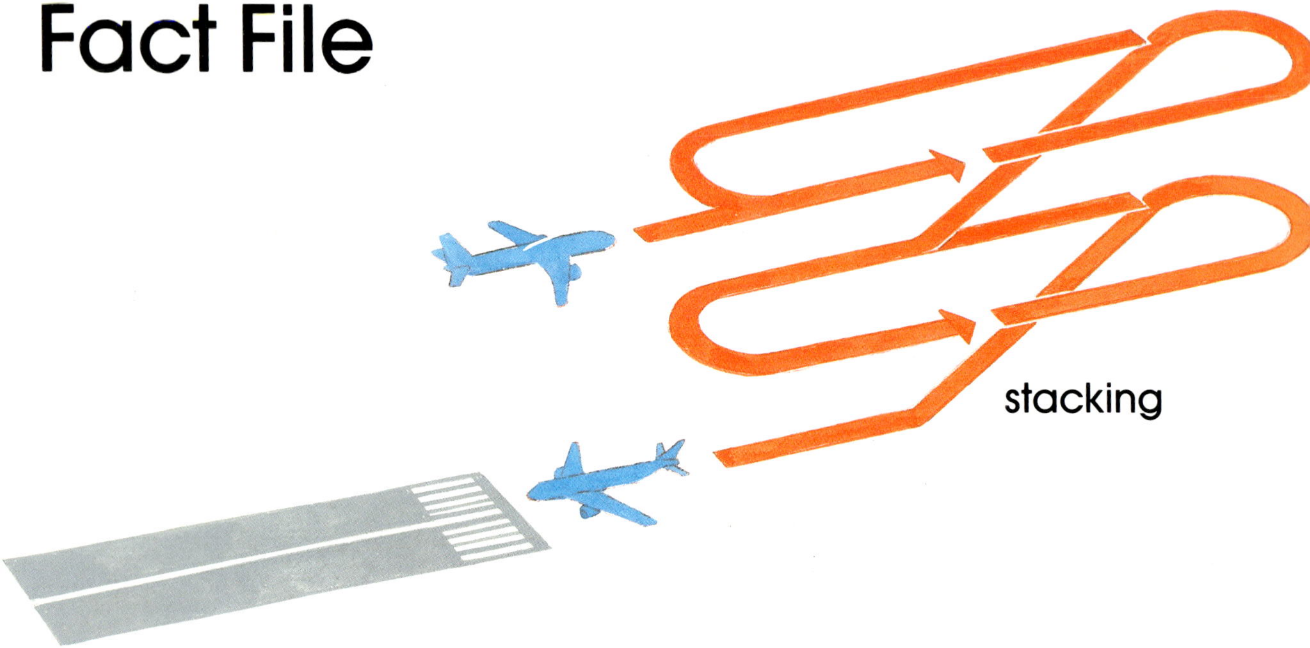

What are the main parts of an airport?
There are four main parts of an airport. These are the **terminal**, the **control tower**, the **runways** and the **hangars**.

How do planes know when it is safe to take off?
The control tower tells the pilot. The controllers can see the runways. They can see all the planes for miles around on their radar screens. They know when there is a runway free. They know when the plane's route is clear.

How do planes know when to land?
As planes approach the airport, they ask if they can land. Often they have to wait. The control tower tells them to circle. The planes circle one above the other. This is called stacking. When there is room for a plane to

land, the control tower tells the plane at the bottom of the stack to land.

What happens to the planes between airports?

There are ground stations all along a plane's route. The stations send out strong signals which track the planes. Signals from these stations tell the airport where the plane is. In this way, air traffic controllers make sure that the planes keep a safe distance apart. Planes travelling in opposite directions fly at different heights. This means there is no chance of them crashing into each other.

Index